Your Ad Here

De-Mystifying the Business of Media and Advertising

First published by Dog Ear Publishing
4010 W. 86th Street, Ste H
Indianapolis, IN 46268
www.dogearpublishing.net

ISBN: 978-160844-538-7

This book is printed on acid-free paper.

Printed in the United States of America

Table of Contents

Acknowledgements

Both Michael and I thoroughly enjoyed the process of putting this book together. Untold hours have gone into taking a rather complex subject and trying to figure out how to boil it down into simple terms. It sounds easy, doesn't it? When we first started the process, we thought so, too. We even thought it would only take a couple of months to complete! As time has gone by, the project turned into a true labor of love: the love of advertising and media combined with the love of taking a subject that can be very overwhelming and expressing it in a way that will assist those who really want help in building their business. The publishing of this book is the culmination of a dream for both of us and we hope you will find it useful as you continue to build your business.

This project would not have been possible without the help of family, friends, business partners and media affiliates. Thank you to all but most especially to the following people:

- Jaime Frare, Time Warner Cable, for her love of the cable industry and her enthusiastic approach to editing.
- Adam Jones, WCWN, for his explicit notes.
- Zack Brown, Entercom, for understanding what we are trying to do.
- Barry Bryant, Digital Media, for his patience http://massmediamobile.blogspot.com/.
- Matt Duddy, Lamar, for his insightful remarks and added information.
- David Weinstein, Vox Design, and Melissa Ward, New Ward Development, for fine tuning and added information.
- Tracy Lewis, Times Union Newspapers, for fact checking and insightful comments.
- Shelle Fitzsimmons, MNI, for noticing that the math didn't add up.

We also want to extend a special thank you to:
- Jason McIntosh, Crosshairs Graphics, for the cover design and illustrations www.5dcreative.com. We're so happy with the outcome.
- Carlene Pavlak, for those long evenings of editing, commenting and help in putting the glossary together. Wow, that was a tough job! We owe you.
- Matt Martindale and Christofer VanWormer from Egolabel.com for our stellar website. As usual, you guys did a fantastic job.

We would appreciate any comments that you might have as you read through these pages. You can email either one of us directly at our website address <u>www.YourAdHereTheBook.com</u>. Please enjoy the book and the services we are providing on our website. We wish you all the best.

Introduction

Media and advertising is everywhere. It's a huge part of our culture. Turn on your computer screen and it is likely there will be a figure gyrating across your screen trying to sell you an online college degree or low rate auto loan. Open the newspaper and even within the columns of news you'll see ads for everything from divorce lawyers to dance studios to funeral homes. Pull out of your driveway and onto the highway and more than likely you'll notice billboards promoting the latest craft festival or maybe the latest cell phone technology. Flick on your radio and you may hear an ad for your local dry cleaner that reminds you that you left your laundry hanging over the kitchen chair. Settle in for an evening at home in front of the television and once again, you'll be offered the opportunity to purchase everything from fast food to a shiny new car to some microwave popcorn. Check your messages on your phone and there may be a text message for the latest sale of Crazy Boy Jeans. It's everywhere. So how do you get *your* message heard in all the noise?

The media and advertising business is a mystery to most people. Even account reps from one media to the next may not fully understand how the other works. Broadcast and outdoor are two very different animals with a different set of parameters and calculations. Media buyers work in an environment of long mathematical calculations and believe us when we tell you; they put a lot of trust in their gut. So how are you supposed to know where to start when many professionals are quite often in the dark?

Well, you started in the right place. "Your Ad Here, De-mystifying the Business of Media and Advertising" came as a result of a meeting that was held one hot and humid August afternoon. I had been asked to create a media analysis for a very large corporation that suspected there was a problem with their media placements. I have a myriad of business background, but analysis is my real forte and media is secondary. Realizing that I needed help to complete the project, I elicited the help of Michael because I've worked with him for a number of years now and know first hand that he is a media geek. Some might even call him a media guru. After presenting the project and seeing the grateful expression on the face of the media specialist, I called Michael and said, "We need to meet." Out of that project came the outline for this book.

With the help of some local media experts and support of our truly good friends and family, we have put together what we believe is the most simplified nuts and bolts version of how to buy media that is out there today. We have laid the book out in two sections for your ease of use. Section One includes the actual process to follow for targeting your audience, planning your budget, contacting your account executive, sending your availability requests, compiling the data, trafficking your buys and an overview about the creative. Section Two includes a chapter on cable, broadcast, outdoor, digital media, word of mouth marketing, radio, print, value added, yellow pages and media production. With the detail we've provided, it won't take long until you are maximizing the success of your message.

We've also provided a glossary of terms that we believe will be very useful. There is a companion website at <u>www. YourAdHere TheBook.com</u> which includes downloadable forms for your use and market information that will be updated constantly. We also want you to know that we are at your service if you have questions or want more detailed help with your planning and buying. We've even included some entertaining stories of the crazy things that have happened in our own experiences of media and advertising. We hope you enjoy those as well.

So now it's up to you. Read the book, follow the process and start negotiating. It won't be long until your message will begin to be heard. We have referenced our website in each chapter so please use it often if you have questions or even want to share your own successes.

Both Michael and I wish you the best in your business ventures. Your purchase of this book takes us one step closer to our own kind of success! Win-win is a beautiful thing.

Note: To make things a little easier, words that are **bolded** throughout the chapters can be found in the Glossary.

SECTION ONE

Getting Started

CHAPTER ONE

Targeting Your Audience

Figuring out exactly who it is that would be interested in your product or service is one of the very first things you'll need to determine. Exactly who is your audience?   Are you selling a product or service that is targeting soccer moms, middle-aged women, males age 18-34, affluent professionals? What we hear often is, "Well, really everybody *might* be my audience." Many businesses are not sure of who their target is so you're not alone if you're in that group. It's our goal to help you start figuring that out.

The first thing you're going to want to do is to take the time to look over your receipts, email inquiries, sales, store traffic, consulting practice, whatever your case may be. Ask yourself some questions. You can start with the questions we've listed. As you get into the process, we're sure you'll think of more.

1. Are there more males, females or is it an even mix that buys your product or uses your service?
2. Into what age group do your clients fit? Common age demos include:

   - 18-34
   - 25-54
   - 18-49
   - 25-49

3. When they come to your place of business are they driving, walking or do they take public transportation?
4. As a rule, how do they communicate with you? Do they call on the phone, email, write a letter, IM, or do they come in person?
5. Are they executives, middle management, blue collar workers, moms, college students, young kids, or maybe they're unemployed?

It may be difficult for you smaller business people to take the time to work through this exercise. But you need to do it. Here's a suggestion for you. You can always elicit the help of a local college intern. Many schools are looking for placement for business and marketing students to do just this type of project. Be creative. Use your resources. They are there. And just think about what a great learning experience this would be for a "fresh face" marketing student. It's yet another opportunity for the win-win that we will emphasize all through this book.

Once you've completed this exercise, you will have a basic idea of who you are trying to speak to with your advertising.

The key here is to focus in on your core audience. An example of finding focus for your audience might be that of any national fast food chain. These chains have targeted the average American with 2.5 kids that eat out at least once or twice per week. Advertising messages are delivered close to meal times in places where the fast food chain's target audience is likely to hear it or see it. Of course these large chains also have the benefit of huge budgets which allow them to focus in even further with different creative ads. But you can learn more about targeting your audience by paying attention to when and where you see their ads. There's a lot to learn there.

Once you have built your marketing profile and you understand who your target audience is, the next step is to focus in on your geographic boundaries. Is your product a local product? Or would your market be regional, national or even international? Think about where you are today in your business and where you'd like to be in a few years. Don't be afraid to dream, but for now, keep it real.

Okay, so you've looked at your market and you've given some thought about where you'd like to be in the future. The next step is to build a quick **Target Profile** using the information you've found. A target profile is a simple statement of who you believe your audience is. It will consist of age demographic, male, female or both, how they communicate to you, and geographic boundary. Rest assured that the media account executive is going to ask you about this. They want to understand how they can help and this information will be the basis of what they provide you.

So let's say for the sake of discussion that your target is young adults both male and female between the ages of 18 and 30 who rely on public transportation and most of your sales from them have come through a website or by some other digital means. Using that bit of information, your account executive can do a bit of primary research for you to find out helpful information such as how long these folks spend commuting, what other internet sites they visit and even what other products they may purchase in the next six months.

By taking the time to really focus in on your target, you have just saved yourself both time and money. You now know who you're targeting, where they live, how they spend their money and with that information, you can make the best media buying choices.

This is a basic approach that we are suggesting. If you need help or would like suggestions about honing in on your target group, please feel free to contact us at <u>www.YourAdHereThe Book.com</u>. We're happy to help.

So now you know who you want to talk to, let's get you ready to plan!

CHAPTER TWO

Planning Your Budget

Okay, so now you know who your target audience is and it's time for you to start figuring out how much you would like to spend to get their attention. This is a very important part of the process in getting your message heard. Be assured that the first question any media representative is going to ask you whether he or she is selling print, broadcast, cable, outdoor, radio, digital or even yellow pages will be, "So how much is your budget for the campaign?" It can be an intimidating question if you haven't thought about it so give your budget serious consideration before you begin reaching out to any media outlets. Planning a budget, just like targeting your market, is the cornerstone to your ad campaign. In this chapter we're going to supply you some general guidelines that should help you figure out what you can afford to spend.

If you're a small or start-up company, you may not have advertised at all beyond the Yellow Pages. Your company is doing fine but it's not growing the way you'd like. You want to advertise but you're not sure how to measure your results. To you, marketing or advertising is like throwing your money up into the air on a windy day and hoping that it will come back to you. Up until now you may have relied completely on word of mouth and you've done pretty well but you'd like to do better. You're unsure of what to do because you don't know how to decide how much to spend or how to spend it. You're not even sure you can afford to advertise. But in today's competitive economy, the real question is, can you afford *not* to advertise?

We'll make this as simple as we can for you. The benchmark for budgeting is to plan on spending 1% to 5% of your gross sales on advertising and media.

Using this example, if your gross sales are $1 million, you could comfortably spend $10,000 to $50,000. Of course, that's great for an established company that has a sound handle on sales and marketing. But let's face it; many small and start-up businesses don't have a track record that is helpful for budgeting purposes. In these cases it'll be a personal decision to spend what is comfortable for you. You'll have to estimate based on cash on hand and projected revenue. The old adage that you have to spend money to make money still holds true today but not if it digs in too deep to your operating cash. You'll need to plan carefully and place your ads where you can really optimize your results. And the key word here is SPEND. Whatever you decide to budget for your campaign, stick with it and make it happen.

A good place to start is by doing a little homework. Using this book and the companion website, you can get a good handle on the cost of media in your area. Go ahead and dream big. Check out all of your resources but keep one thing mind; when money is an issue, spreading too little into too many media avenues will severely dilute your message. Do yourself a favor and read each chapter of this book carefully. Once you've done that, then decide where you'd like to start. There is so much available to you. Use every possible resource. We've tried to keep the reading light and informational so it shouldn't be too tough for you to get through it all.

Also keep in mind that some really creative advertising campaigns have been carried out on a shoe string budget. One example we came across recently was of a small gaming company that has chalked up their marketing success to a combination of "common sense and creative ideas". Their promotional strategy focused on word of mouth and giving bloggers and the media something to write about. Look at your business and think creatively. Use your imagination and ask yourself if there something you're doing that the local media might find interesting. Or maybe the users of your product would like to comment on your blog. Take every interview opportunity you can get and send out free copies of the interview to anyone who asks for it and maybe even to those who don't ask but who you think may find it interesting and possibly useful. Post it on your website and get people talking about it. For more on this type of marketing, take a look at the chapter on Word of Mouth Marketing in Section 2. At this writing Word of Mouth marketing is the big thing for smaller companies to get their products and services the attention they need on a shoestring budget.

And here's something we'd like you to think about. We have a friend who once told his dentist, "I don't drill my own teeth so why do you your own advertising?" So much truth is spoken in jest, isn't it? But the bottom line here is, go to the experts. They're there to help. If you succeed, they succeed. Win-win is a beautiful thing.

This book and the companion website are great resources in helping you plan your budget. Of course if you have questions or need any individual help, we're here. Feel free to contact us at www.YourAdHereTheBook.com.

CHAPTER THREE

Contacting Your Account Executive

The first step you'll be taking once you have a media budget and a buying strategy is to contact media account executives. This book is going to save you the aggravation of contacting these execs directly by providing you with a little but very effective short cut since we all know that efficient use of time is the best use of time.

Please take note of what we're going to say next: *Do not call the station or media property if you can avoid it.*

Making the initial contact by phone can be a very draining experience. You don't want that. So instead of picking up the phone to the media outlet, dial a fellow marketer or a business associate and ask them who they work with at each outlet. Or you can go to the website and pick an email address of the sales staff. Please do not use the info@ address since it's not reliable.

If you're working from a referral, you can send an introductory email that says something like this:

> *"Subject: Referral*
>
> *Text: Hello. My associate Chrissie VanWormer from M&V Media recommended you as one of the best media representatives out there. We are considering including WXYZ for our fall campaign and I would like to send you an Availability Request/Request for Information we have prepared. (We'll get to this in the next chapter.) This is merely a preliminary phase and as of yet have not determined our buy parameters or the stations we will use. I will send the request over on (insert date here) and would appreciate it if you would please confirm receipt."*

This approach will give the clear message that you will not be accepting unsolicited phone calls. Media representatives are great people but it is their purpose to make a sale. They are organized, driven and motivated to succeed. Add to that they have sales managers yelling, prodding them toward the door, repeating over and over again to follow-up, follow-up, follow-up. Plus they have weekly sales meetings at which they have to state their success in front of everyone. If they can honestly say, "Look, the customer instructed me not to call. If I don't hear from her next week, I will follow-up with a phone call. If I call before then, I might jeopardize the sale."

In the event that you don't happen to know anyone who is using the local media outlets and you're not sure who to call, ask for the voice mail of the local sales manager at each outlet. Most media outlets have contact information right on their websites. If the local sales manager's information is not stated clearly, you can go ahead and just pick someone. The person who receives the call will forward it on to the appropriate person. You can leave a message something like this:

> *"Hi Mr. Local Sales Representative. My name is Tom Smith from Crazy Boy Jeans. I have an availability request/request for information that I would like to send over to you. My email address is (insert address here) and my phone number is (insert number here). The best time to reach me is (insert time here)."*

One of two things will happen. First, you may get a call back from the sales manager who will be looking for more information. You can say,

> *"It is outlined in the availability request/request for information. I will be happy to send it to you in whatever way is most convenient for you."*

Or you may get a call from the account executive that has been assigned to the account. Be assured that the account executive will ask you the very same questions. In that case, you say the same thing as noted above.

It is not our intention to scare you or make you think the media account executives are big scary ogres that you need to ward off. Not in the least. They can be a great advocate for your business and they want to help. If your business succeeds, they succeed. It's win-win. But they are trained to ask many questions that you may not be ready to answer. Some of these questions may even be intimidating if you are new to media buying. Your job at this point is to be cordial and respectful but mostly importantly, it is your job to get the contact information you need.

If you'd like any more information on contacting your account executive, we can help. You can contact us through our website at <u>www.YourAdHereTheBook.com</u>.

CHAPTER FOUR

Sending Out an Availability Request

So you've done your initial research and you're feeling pretty good about it. Your media database is becoming a living breathing thing; its DNA built of television stations, radio, print commodities including newspapers and magazines and outdoor including billboards, gas tank toppers, etc. You're ready to go. The next step is sending out an **availability request (avail request)**.

So what is an avail request? Very simply put it is a request for information. You will be asking what is available from each media outlet during the specific time frame you have chosen. Each media outlet will provide you the information you will need to make an informed media buy.

Your avail request should include your name, date, contact email and phone. Don't forget to include the media outlet name and the account executive name you received while building your database. Something that basic now and again gets forgotten! The body of the avail request will supply details on the information you require and very importantly, a deadline for submission.

Why do you need an avail request? Why can't you just call the media representative and start asking questions? Well, you can go ahead and do that if you don't want to be taken seriously. Sending an official avail request gives you much more credibility. Plus a well planned document is much easier for the representative to follow. He or she will know exactly what it is you are looking to accomplish. Beyond that, it makes tracking so much easier. You will have the dates you sent the avail request to the outlets, who you sent it to and who submitted the information back to you. This will be very helpful in tracking and planning and later for billing purposes.

How do you put together an avail request? It may seem a little overwhelming if you've never done it before so we've included a template for your use on our website at www.YourAdHere TheBook.com. But you'll need to know how to fill it out. Each media type has a unique set of parameters so we'll need to spend some time on each. Once you understand them, you'll feel much more confident when it comes time to place your buy.

Let's start with Radio. Radio is measured by Arbitron, a media and marketing research firm serving the media outlets as well as advertisers and ad agencies in the United States. It publishes its reports four times each year after taking measurements in winter, spring, summer and fall. These sought after reports are referred to as "books". All you really need to know in order to make good use of this information is that "books" is a survey that details all the listeners and station information in any given market.

When considering radio, there are a few key parameters to help you in your analysis. First there is **Average Quarter Hour**

(AQH) which will tell you how many people are listening for at least five minutes in any fifteen minute block. The second key parameter is **Daypart.** Daypart is simply a part of the day. Standard dayparts are:

- AM drive (6A-10A)
- MidDay (10A-3P)
- PM drive (3P-7P)
- Evenings (7P-12A)
- Weekends

Next is **Cumulative Audience (Cume)** and no we're not talking about your college grades. Cume is the total number of listeners in a given week who make up the market in which you will be placing your advertising. The last key parameter you'll want to consider is **Ratings.** Ratings is the percentage of the total *listening* audience as compared to the entire *possible* listening audience.

You will most likely receive your information as decimals (ratings) and actual numbers (000's). The ratings will allow you to compute the **Gross Rating Points (GRPs)** of your plan. We will bore you with an explanation of gross rating points and why they are so important a little later. For our purposes here, the (000's) are probably more appropriate for what we're talking about as it will give you the total number of listeners.

Let's move on to Broadcast Television and Cable. One of the key parameters would, of course, be **Time Period.** Standard television time periods are:

- Early AM (5A-7A)
- Early AM News (7A-9A)
- Daytime (9A-3P)
- Early Fringe (3P-5P)
- Early News (5P-7P)
- Prime Access (7P-8P)
- Prime (8P-11P)

- Late News (11P-11:35P)
- Late Fringe (11:35P-1:30A)

We've included a sample TV programming grid for you on our website. This will help you understand how a station or property schedules the time periods.

Television, like radio, is rated four times each year although the ratings are done at different times. We've all heard the term "sweeps", right? Television "sweeps" are done in February, May, July and November. Depending on the time of your campaign, you will want to see numbers that most closely mirror that time of the programming year. For example, if your campaign will be in April, you will want to see actual numbers from May of the previous year. This will give you an historical indication of how the program or time period did in the same slot during the same season.

Outdoor or Out of Home as it is sometimes called is measured in **Showings**. Showings are a group of outdoor boards which will provide a certain percentage coverage of a market. There are two types of outdoor postings; bulletins and posters. Bulletins are the large expressway postings normally made of vinyl which makes them re-useable. Posters are the smaller local roadway postings. It's a poster you'll occasionally see de-faced with a moustache or graffiti. Luckily, they are made of paper which makes them easy to replace plus, in comparison to vinyl, they are inexpensive.

Be sure to ask your outdoor media representative for a map of locations in the geographic area you are thinking of using. These maps are readily available and will aid you in finding the best location for your artwork.

Print is purchased **Per Column Inch**. This concept can seem confusing but is actually simple. Here's an example. If your ad is $21.00 per column inch and you run a 15 column inch ad, your cost is $315. ($21 x 15 = $315) The parameters for print are basic. It's all about **Circulation.** Circulation is the number of papers/magazines delivered on a weekly basis and is measured for accuracy by the **Audit Bureau of Circulation (ABC)**. The ABC is a non-profit circulation auditing organization. It is one of the several organizations operating in different parts of the world that audits circulation, readership, and audience information for the magazines, newspapers and other publications produced by their members.

All types of print, including magazines, often use the term **Readership** as part of their measurements. Readership is not just the number of papers/magazines sold but it takes into account that not everyone reads the publication and then immediately drops it into the recycle bin. Studies have shown that in most cases 2.1 persons will pick up and read the publication before it is finally disposed of. Be sure to get this piece of information from your print publication and use it in your analysis.

Each medium discussed above is covered in detail in its own chapter in this book. If you are confused, please go to the appropriate chapter and read it carefully before sending out your avail request. The chapters are easy to read and easy to understand but if you have more questions, please contact us at www.YourAdHereTheBook.com for clarification.

CHAPTER FIVE

Compiling the Data

You've got your contact list complete. You've sent out your avail request and now your email box has been deluged with information and attachments. Most of the stations responded by the deadline but if any missed the due date, you'll want to give them a call to follow up. (This is not a common occurrence but it does happen.)

As you've received your information you've printed out all the **Portable Document Formats (PDF)**, station details, Excel spreadsheets, Power Point presentations and Word documents. Unfortunately there is no standard response format to make the whole process just a bit simpler. Some documents will look similar but others will look completely different. The pile in front of you looks a little daunting so you're going to need to figure out a way to organize the information to make it a little less overwhelming. We're going to help you make this as simple as possible.

Experience has shown us that a simple, old-fashioned three ring binder is one of the best solutions out there. Divide it by market (if you're doing a large buy), by media and by station. Lay it out in the fashion that makes it easiest for you to simplify and understand the information you've received. Only you know what will work best for you.

There is another option out there that we recently came across and are using for our clients. It's a software portal called Avenue Right that gathers and manages all of the data and avail requests for buyers and planners. You can check them out at AvenueRight.net.

Once you're comfortable, it's time to start setting up your **Media Calendar**. A media calendar can be a simple Excel spreadsheet but it will make the buying process much easier. The media calendar will show you in one clear, concise snapshot everything you're doing for your advertising campaign.

Your media calendar will denote:

- Stations
- Dayparts
- Programming
- Ratings
- Reach
- Frequency
- Creative

Each of these categories will be explained as we continue explaining the process for a quick referral, check the glossary in the back of the book or you can go to www.YourAdHereThe Book.com for explanation.

Keep in mind that across all media types and outlets, broadcast weeks run from Monday through Sunday. In order to keep things clear between you and your media representative, you'll want to lay out your plan in this manner. Using a media calendar is a great tool for checking your consistency across media outlets so make a habit of using it. We've included a sample media calendar that is a downloadable PDF at our website.

CHAPTER SIX

Trafficking Your Buys

Okay, so now the schedules are done, your ad spots are placed, some **Value Added** has been negotiated and an **Insertion Order** sent, signed and returned. So now you can sit back and wait for the business to start coming in, right? Wrong. You've got to place your traffic instructions.

Traffic is a standard term that tells the media outlet what copy or ad spot to run. It can be a separate document or it can be included on the insertion order. There is really no right or wrong way to send it. Experience will tell you what works best for you. What is important is that you keep track of how you placed your traffic. The document, however you decided to place it, is the one document that will let you know whether or not your buy was run as ordered. And don't forget to hang on to it because you will need a copy of those traffic instructions when it comes time to reconcile your order to the invoice.

Here is a sample traffic instruction using Crazy Boy Jeans as an example. Their traffic instructions may have looked something like this:

- Client: Crazy Boy Jeans
- Date: 00/00/00
- Flight Dates: April 1 through May 31
- Copy Rotation:
    - "Crazy Boy Jeans 50% Off Sale" : 30 25%
    - "Crazy Boy Jeans Branding" : 30 25%
    - "Crazy Boy Tween Jeans" : 30 20%
    - "Crazy Boy Summer Shorts" : 30 30%

Please remember that you'll have to run percentages in a whole number format. In other words, you'll be unable to traffic your spots with instructions that use numbers like 31.5%, 33.35%, 68%. All placements should be in units of 5 or 10 and add up to 100.

Once again we've included a sample Traffic Instruction document on our website www.YourAdHereTheBook.com.

CHAPTER SEVEN

About the Creative

If we've done our job as well as we hope we did, we've cleared up some of the mystery for you about how media and advertising works. It's not an easy concept to understand but we believe we've boiled it down pretty well.

However, as we were reading over our final edits, we realized that you're probably wondering how you come up with all these great ideas for logos, ideas for advertising campaigns, etc. We're also sure you've seen a number of television shows over the years that glamorize the ad creation business. We're here to assure you that it's really not like that at all. In fact, it's just as methodical as any other business discipline. You'll need to start by asking yourself a few questions just like you did when you were trying to figure out how to target your market and plan your budget.

As you're trying to figure this out, you'll want to consider a few things such as:

- What is your company's image? Are you casual, corporate, fun, serious?

- Is your current campaign going to include a timeless ad that can be re-used and re-purposed for other media such as a direct mail or a radio script or is it going to be a short term blast?

- Is it something that will span multiple media platforms including television, cable, print, radio and web or will it only apply to one media?

Asking yourself these questions will help you begin to plan how to craft your company image.

Another useful tool may be to do a simple **SWOT Analysis** in which you'll identify your Strengths, Weaknesses, Opportunities and Threats. Be honest and really give it thought. It can be a revealing process.

This can be a significant amount of work and an overwhelming process. We are currently working on a book that will break this all down just a simply as we've broken down media for you. Keep your eyes opened for it as it will be on bookshelves shortly.

In the meantime, please feel free to contact us at <u>www.YourAd HereTheBook.com</u> for help in planning. We know some great creative people and are happy to make recommendations.

SECTION TWO

How To Do It

Cable

Let's recap. So far you've contacted your media representatives and you've built yourself a database of stations. You drafted a killer avail request and have received all the media submissions that you need. You organized the data in a media binder that will help you in your upcoming buy. So that part is finished. Now the fun begins. It's time to negotiate the **Schedules.** The schedules are a plan that identifies the media channels used in advertising campaigns. The schedules specify insertion or broadcast dates, positions and duration of the messages.

At this point, negotiating the schedules probably sounds more like an episode of some scary reality shows on one of the stations you're about to buy. Believe us when we say, "Have no fear." We're here to walk you through the process and make it a win-win for everyone.

The first thing to keep in mind about the negotiating is that each person has his or her own priorities. You want to get the most media exposure for your company that you can possibly get with the money you have to spend. The account executive on the other hand, has a goal to sell the station's inventory at the best possible price for the station. He or she knows the competitors in the area and wants to win a portion of the budget for the company they are representing.

It's at this point that we really want to emphasize how important it is to understand and empathize with the account executive. It is their job to make you happy and help you succeed but they have a job to do as well. It is up to you to be respectful while you are pounding out the best deal possible.

The first step in the media negotiating process is to know your own "walk away" position. Figure out in your own mind what is the most you are willing to pay for a spot, a schedule or a posting. You know your budget. You know your goals. If you set up a simple line item chart for each media, you'll be sure not to stray outside of those parameters.

For example, let's say you have $50,000 to spend. Your chart may look something like this:

- Outdoor/Out of Home $10,000
- Broadcast TV $ 7,000
- Cable TV $10,000
- Digital: $10,000
- Radio $ 3,000
- Print $ 5,000
- Incremental $ 5,000

Let's start with cable TV. You'll first want to determine whether you will be using fifteen second (:15) or thirty second (:30) spots. Typically a fifteen second spot will cost 75% of the price of a thirty second spot.

Cable is sold by the entire interconnect (the complete geographic subscriber area) or zone (zip code, cities or counties). If you are an advertiser who wants to hit everyone in your market, then you should use the interconnect. That is the broad base of the entire area. However, if you have a limited retail range, zoned advertising is your best bet. It's clear, it's concise and you'll know exactly who it is you're reaching.

So now you've made a couple of key decisions. You know who is it you're trying to reach (everyone or a smaller specific clientele) and what your format will be (:15 or :30). The key to buying cable is to mix your **Reach Networks** with **Frequency Networks**. Reach networks are the larger audience networks which tend to be more popular such as ESPN, USA, TNT and TBS. Frequency networks on the other hand have a smaller audience base with niche programming. Some examples are Food, HGTV, MTV, WE, FX.

You'll also want to have a mix of broad dayparts. (As we discussed earlier, dayparts are simply the parts of the day your ads will run in). The broad dayparts will consist of time frames such as Monday through Sunday 7p-12A. Add to this some fixed time periods such as Monday 9P-10P, Tuesday, Thursday 8P-10P. The reasoning behind this approach is to speak to the niche viewer, the appointment TV viewer and the elusive guys sitting in front of their TV with the remote control repeatedly hitting the up and down arrow, running through the channels. Yes, those guys really can be "caught" and this is exactly how you'll do it.

The nice thing about using this approach of reach and frequency/broad and niche view is that this is doable, it's easy and it's affordable.

Now you want to figure out how to spend your budget. If your budget is for long term marketing messaging, you may want to place it to run one week on and then one week off. In this case a full month of funds could run over eight weeks giving you a greater reach. If your message is for a short term blast such as a retail sale with a finite period, you'll want to figure that into your messaging as well.

Start by setting your weekly budget and a weekly spot goal. Think about how you would like this to run. For example:

- Weekly Expenditure: $2,500
- Weekly Spot Goal: 35 spots
- Average Cost Per Spot: $71
  ($2,500 / 35 spots = $71 average cost per spot)

By laying your goals out plain and simple, you'll have your own boundaries to work within. However, in the initial discussions with your account executive, *it is important not to share too much budget detail.* It is perfectly acceptable to say something like,

"I've got in the range of $8-$12 K for this campaign."

Now let's move on to the actual negotiating. Work on the reach networks first. The demand for the reach networks is higher so as you might expect, the pricing is higher as well. Set yourself a benchmark rule of thumb for negotiating off of the submitted rates. Keep in mind there is more room for negotiation in the first quarter when there is less demand for the inventory. You may get an agreement right away or the account executive might say,

"What if I do ESPN for $____?" If you're comfortable with that, then accept and move on. If not, try this response, *"I can't really do that. Could you open up the time period to ______ and ______ for ____?"*

Opening up a time period refers to widening the time of day. For example, you've received pricing for 6A-9A and you might want to widen it to 5A-10A which is opening up the time slot by two hours. In many cases, this will drop the prices enough to agree on. Remember to be reasonable in the price you're offering. This will speed up negotiations and cut down on frustration felt not only by you but by your account executive. (Tips for negotiating can be found at our website www.YourAdHere TheBook.com. Periodic updates are available. Check the site often!)

Continue the same approach with all of the reach networks. Once that task is complete, you'll move on to your frequency networks. Use the same approach there as well. It is important to clearly state what you want, you can say,

> *"Is this your best rate? I have a deadline to meet and I'd like us both to make the best use of our time."*

So you've done it. Congratulations! You got the rates you needed within the budget parameters you set and it's win-win for everybody. Now you're going to want to send an insertion order to complete the task.

An insertion order is a document that outlines everything you agreed upon and becomes your contract with the media outlet. It includes start and end dates of each flight, the name of the campaign, billing information and a signature line. Don't worry; you don't need to figure out how to put one of these together because you can download one from our website. Fill it out; then email or fax it over to the account executive. Be sure you get a signed copy back for your records. As stated above, this signed document will be the contract between you and the media outlet. They need to agree to run the schedule as you noted in the order. It is VERY IMPORTANT to be sure this is done since when the invoice arrives, it will be the insertion order that you will refer to when reconciling the order to the invoice.

For more information on purchasing cable, please contact us at www.YourAdHereTheBook.com.

CHAPTER NINE

Broadcast

You've scored big with cable and now you're beginning to feel a bit more confident in your understanding of how this all works. Now it's time to move on to broadcast. Go back to your initial budget and see what you've set as figure for broadcast television. Broadcast television is expensive so it will be important to really hone in on your audience. You'll need to decide if you want to cast a wide net which simply means shoot the ad out there for everyone *or* if you want to talk to a very specific part of your target audience.

What we're going to say next is very important. Consider the point carefully before you decide how you're going to spend your broadcast funds:

Keep in mind that the audience you are trying to reach may not necessarily be watching the same programming that you enjoy.

Before you contact your account executive, the one thing that you should have decided is your daypart distribution. Now remember that a daypart is a span of time that you'd like your ad to be seen in. Are you thinking you'd like your message in the local news, in daytime talk shows, in prime programming, late news or late night? Keep in mind that your choice of time period is directly related to WHO you are trying to talk to…your target audience. Consider the following few general facts as you're making this decision.

- Professionals tend to tune into news products.
- Affluent individuals are inclined to prime time and late night programming.
- You're more likely to catch soccer moms in daytime and talk shows.

Remember this is only generally the way you'll catch these busy people. Your account executive can help you find the best way to hone in on your target audience.

Another very important fact to remember is that everything we are stating here is based in very broad terms. Each market and each campaign is completely unique. Your media account executive can help determine the course that is right for you.

The next order of business is looking at rating points. Let's say for instance that you're considering a national show such as the "Today Show" which delivers a four (4) rating for your target group. (A rating of 4 indicates that 4% of the total viewing audience is tuned in during that time slot.) Your local media outlet will be looking at several factors in the negotiating process.

- They'll consider how the show is **Trending**. The term trending is just a fancy way of asking for a measurement showing whether the program is losing or gaining audience.

- They'll also be using projections. The projections come from a formula that takes a number from one survey period and multiplies it by a number from a different survey to arrive at a projected rating. This really isn't an easy concept to grasp so we've provided formulas for your use at our website.
- Lastly they'll be considering inventory availability for the time period you are considering. **Inventory Availability** in broadcast can be compared to shelf space offered to vendors by your local supermarket or the number of televisions that can be placed in a store like Best Buy or Sears. In broadcast, inventory availability equals the amount of spots available to purchase at a specified price in a specified time period.

You'll want to be armed with as much information as possible going into the negotiation. When you send out your avail request, you will most likely ask for the survey book that most closely mirrors the time that your campaign is to run. If you're considering an April campaign, then the survey book you would ask for might be the May book from the previous year. You're probably wondering why you would want to look at last year's information as a frame of reference for a new campaign. If you think about it, things like weather, holidays and other type of events remain constant each year. It's a good idea to compare that way.

Let's use the "Today Show" to get you started. Please keep in mind that every market is different and there is no standard pricing anywhere. We'll look at what might be the snapshot of a mid-size television market. A mid-sized market might be a market the size of the Albany, NY and would probably contain households as outlined below:

- 500,000 TV HH (Televisions per household)
- 4% of those households are watching the "Today Show"
- 20,000 viewers could see your message with one thirty second spot
  (500,000 X .04 = 20,000)

Most morning news shows will likely be priced in the $200 to $400 range for a thirty second spot. How many should you buy and at what cost? You'll want to start by allocating your broadcast budget by time period. For example, consider that your target is affluent professionals. We've discussed that target group as tuning in to news, prime and late night programming. Armed with this information, you may consider breaking your budget out as follows:

- Early morning: $2,000
- Prime" $6,000
- Late night: $2,000

The negotiating process is the same as it is for cable and radio. Using the techniques in this book and at <u>www.YourAdHereThe Book.com</u>, you and your account executive will agree on a mutually acceptable price. Let's say at the end of a successful negotiation that you've placed ten spots on the "Today Show". Congratulations! You've just reached 200,000 viewers.

Continue using the same process for late night. Late night programming generally yields a rating of 2. In a medium sized market, that would equate to 2% of the televisions per household or 10,000 viewers. (500,000 x .02 = 10,000). Negotiate carefully, choose wisely and you can easily reach over 100,000 viewers with your budget.

We saved prime time for last quite honestly because it is a little trickier than the other dayparts. **Prime Time** is the part of the daily broadcast time during which the number of listeners or viewers is the highest. There is a huge difference in how each of the local affiliates price prime time. *Remember, it's pure economics: supply and demand.* There are more advertisers wanting advertising time during prime (thus the name PRIME) which drives the price up. Most of what is called "A" prime is just too pricey for the average company's budget. We don't even have to know where you live; with a budget like we're using for an example, there's no discussion. "A" prime broadcast is likely out of your budget. However, don't just assume you can't afford it. Always ask for rates because now and again there may be available space that you can get inexpensively.

So now you're going to want to turn your focus to "B" and "C" prime. These are not the big "buzz" worthy shows but they are still delivering a good audience.   Suffice it to say, with an average prime cost of $650 per spot and an estimated prime ratings delivery of 5 (5% of the viewing audience), you'll get just about 225,000 viewers.

So there you have it, using the techniques we've provided and the resources we offer, you just got yourself 550,000 viewers. That's not bad! For more information and tips on negotiating broadcast television, feel free to contact us at www.YourAdHere TheBook.com. We've got all kinds of tips up our sleeves!

CHAPTER TEN

Outdoor

Outdoor is an interesting animal. The term Outdoor refers to advertising on billboards or signboards generally outside of a building. It is one of those mediums that what we continue to call "traditional" media but it has embraced the digital age by offering digital placements. You've seen those big boards along some of the main interstates changing creative every six seconds. They're bold, beautiful and a great way to get your message heard. It appears that outdoor is not facing the same challenge of declining readership/circulation/listenership, etc. that other mediums are struggling with. Add to that the fact that outdoor audiences circle around the boards while other media circle around the audience trying to get their attention during a specific time and place. The boards are there 24 hours a day seven days a week providing their information whenever you drive by. And it's a great way to layer your advertising.

The first thing you'll need to know is that there are two types of boards: **Bulletins** and **Posters**. Let's start with bulletins. Bulletins are the large units generally found in and around city centers and along freeways. The size varies somewhat but usually will be in the range of 14 feet by 48 feet. The sheer size of bulletins is one of their biggest benefits. It's hard to miss something that big when you're driving to work or to the mall or when you're stuck in traffic. Another big benefit of the bulletin is the fact that they are durable. The creative for these big guys is printed on vinyl which does not disintegrate in the weather and is reusable. Once the vinyl is printed, it can be moved to any board you want, making the message recyclable.

Posters, on the other hand, are generally found on secondary roads and smaller city interchanges. They are printed on paper or on a material known as a flex–poster. Flex-poster is a unique printing process that provides the durability of vinyl with the ease of paper. Most outdoor companies have moved to this process as it has significantly reduced the cost of production by not having to re-order paper anytime someone paints a moustache on your board or writes 'Kirby was here'.

In simple terms when thinking about billboards, consider bulletins as the generals and posters as the soldiers. You'll want to focus on a few bulletins in your area, maybe 20% of your budget mixed with plenty of posters making up the other 80%. And remember, outdoor is all about being big and bold. A billboard's prime reason for existing is to tease your audience. It's not about putting out a wordy message. You'll need to use everything you've got to come up with creative message that tells a story with three or four words and a picture. Do you really need an 800 number on your creative? We don't know about you, but neither of us or anyone we know (we asked!) has ever pulled out a pencil to write down a number as we're buzzing by at 55 miles per hour. The message needs to be short and catchy. Lamar Outdoor recommends seven to ten words. Years of experience has shown that *less is more*. The next time your target audience sees your marketing message on television or hears it on the radio, or sees a digital ad or hears someone talking about you, they'll remember the billboard.

It's all about layering your message. This is just one more piece.

Negotiating outdoor is similar to print in that there is very little room for price negotiation. The rate is the rate. That's just the way it is. When thinking about outdoor, think about it more like the purchase of real estate where the rule of thumb is location, location, location. Price really becomes secondary. It's all about where you want to be seen by the largest concentration of passersby. We're not talking about the largest concentration of passersby in general, but it's more about the largest concentration of passersby who are your target audience. Billboards will have a **Daily Effective Circulation (DEC)** number. DEC is audited by the Traffic Audit Bureau (TAB), an independent source. A DEC number translates to the daily traffic count or how many cars are actually going to drive by your board on any given day. Logic would tell you that you'll want to focus on the higher traffic count boards if you're concentrating on a larger percentage of the population for your product or service.

Your first order of business in buying outdoor is to contact your account executive for a location map. A location map will show the available boards in any area you might be interested in. The first question your account executive will most likely ask you will be "What GRP showing are you interested in seeing?" As we explained earlier, GRP translates to gross rating points and gross rating points simply tells you how much audience is reached with the media choice.

Outdoor is often sold in blocks of 25, 50 and 100 GRPs. This is where you'll really be able to determine how much you can afford. To start, ask for a 25 GRP showing schedule. (25 GRPs means your message will be exposed to 25% of the market audience ages 18+ on a daily basis.) The account executive will provide the map as well as the per board cost. The information you will be provided will give you a very good idea of exactly what you can afford.

All of this is market dependent, but to give you an example of a 25 GRP showing for a medium sized media market, you can use the following calculation as an example. Let's say a 25 GRP showing equals 17 posters at a cost of $750 per poster. This would equal $12,750. Now you'll need to figure in production of two designs which would equal $2,550 in a medium sized market bringing your total to $15,300 for a 2 month commitment.

You smaller business people are probably pulling yourself up off the floor right now so please know that we aren't suggesting you do that. However, buying 5 posters for two 60 day showings will be a well calculated investment of $8,250 and your message will be exposed to a constant stream of traffic for 4 months. Your audience can't shut it off, throw it away or ignore it. It's big, it's bold and with the right creative, it's memorable.

To make this interesting, let's take a look how many people your ad will actually impact with those 5 boards in a medium size market. With an average DEC per board of 12,500 persons multiplied by 5 boards, you will have reached 62,500 possible buyers each day. With a 4 month posting (120 days), you will have made 7,500,000 impressions during the specified period. These numbers are amazing so just think of the impact.

 Here is a piece of advice that will make this purchase a bit easier on both you and the account executive. Don't worry about what we call "cherry picking" board locations until you are ready to sign the agreement. It is a ton of work for the account executive and can be frustrating for both of you. When getting your location maps, ask for the poster and bulletin rates and any package deals that might be available. Most outdoor companies will offer a special deal if you lock up inventory early. Who doesn't want to know in January that a board is sold for the following October? By buying a package deal early, you may get more for your budget than if you're trying to buy individual boards one month at a time.

So there you have it. Once you've gotten the posting and production rates, put them in your media calendar and be sure to set up a reminder for getting your creative to production on time. In most cases, artwork is due two weeks prior to posting. Your account executive will really appreciate not having to hound you as the date for your posting is drawing near.

Numbers and math are based on broad knowledge and do not reflect actual rates in your market. Check out our site www. YourAdHereTheBook.com for more media math and to request a market profile for planning.

CHAPTER ELEVEN

Digital Media
Part A: On the Web

So you're probably wondering exactly what is **Digital Media**? Well, it's new and exciting and changing so rapidly that it's confusing even for a seasoned advertiser. If you decide to look up the Wikipedia definition, your eyes will likely glaze over after the first sentence. Suffice it to say that digital media includes electronic mediums such as website placement, mobile marketing and all wireless technologies. Since we're trying to help you keep your media planning simple, we're going to go start with the basics.

The most sensible place to start seems to be with **Web Placement.** Web placements are the headers, footers and dancers who seem to be gyrating across our screens each time we log in. There are standard sizes that all media properties will adhere to

45

based on the Internet Advertising Bureau (IAB). Those sizes in the world of digital media are known as **Skyscrapers, Leaderboards, Peel Backs** and **Drop Downs**. As you can imagine, skyscrapers are the long, tall placements along the left and right sides of the websites. Makes sense, right? Leaderboards can either be at the top or at the bottom of the page. Peel Backs are the ads that break away from the corner of the page when your mouse is scrolled over it and drop downs are ads that will literally "drop down" as you move your mouse over them. Each of these ad types are considered premium. As such, you will be charged a premium price.

Pricing web ad placement is normally done on a **Cost Per Thousand (CPM)** impressions. A cost per thousand impressions is simply the amount it will cost you to reach 1,000 viewers. To explain that for you, let's say you want to place an ad on your local CBS affiliate website. A skyscraper ad on the site offers a guaranteed delivery of 100,000 impressions served. Sounds impressive, right? But what does it mean? Well, in the world of web advertising what that means is the page will be viewed 100,000 times in a specified period of time. So now let's say you have negotiated a price of $25 CPM. For 100,000 views, your cost will be $2,500. (1,000 * $25 = $2,500) Now, in order to maximize your investment, you'll want to make sure you evenly distribute the impressions over the course of days or weeks. You'll accomplish this by working directly with the account executive at the affiliate and locking down the impressions by daily delivery or site section. If we use the 100,000 impressions on a CBS affiliate as an example, the way you might set that up could look something like this:

- Home Page: 25,000
- Sports: 25,000
- Local News: 25,000
- Weather: 25,000

Based on the metrics that an affiliate such as Commission Junction* provides, the impression delivery for each section could take place within a single day, over the course of a few days or maybe up to a week. It's important that you communicate your goals and needs with the account executive to insure that you get exactly what you need. (*Commission Junction has as its basis performance based marketing which means you'll get paid for customer actions and sales.)

Quite honestly, the best way to know that you're getting the 100,000 impressions is if your web platform will charge you on a **Pay Per Click** basis. Unfortunately, you'll find very few sites that will price out their inventory that way. A pay per click means you'll be charged each time someone "clicks" on your ad bringing them to your site or page. Click through ads will give you a much better indication of the success of your web campaign than impressions "served". So to insure you're getting what you paid for, always ask for the click through rate for every ad position you buy. The site will have the data you need and from there you can determine whether or not you want to continue advertising in that spot or with the web entity at all. There are several sites that will provide comparative click through data free of charge. One of the easiest to use is Compete.com. After a simple sign up, you can compare the impressions delivered of up to three (3) websites at once. More information on Compete.com can be found at our website. We're always on the lookout for more sites like this one so check our site often.

Since we're talking about web advertising, we need to give at least one minute to **Rich Media**. Rich media are the added opportunities web advertising offers. For instance, maybe you have a television spot or a radio ad that you would like to add to your web ad. Or maybe you want to lure potential buyers in with a game they can play that offers a coupon or a higher percentage off merchandise. These opportunities are called rich media. Each one will enrich the experience you are offering your target audience and pique their interest in your product just a bit more than a static (stationary) ad. Add this to the web advertising and you'll see that web placement can and should play a prominent role in your media planning.

Remember the key is *planning* so you'll really need to think about your spending comfort level, how many people you want to reach and how important it is to you to be in the web advertising space. As a benchmark, you might want to commit a minimum of $5,000 to $10,000 total including production and placement to make a real impact. This initial budget is based on an average global cost per thousand of $25. (Keep in mind that the cost per thousand is how much it will cost you to reach 1,000 viewers.) That means that on the high end of this recommendation, you would be reaching 400,000 people. Also please keep in mind that these are averages. You will need to contact your media partners for detailed pricing.

For you smaller business people who are still picking yourselves up off the ground right now after reading those numbers, don't worry. There is another less expensive approach that many people are using with great success. That option is Google AdWords. AdWords provides an easy way to dip your toe into the water of digital advertising without having to dive right in. Start by going to www.AdWords.Google.com. Once there, you'll see it's pretty easy to set up an account, decide your geographic and age targets and design your ad. After you've set up all of those parameters, you'll need to set your budget. Decide how much you want to spend on a daily basis. Let's say for example that you set your budget at $30 per day. Your costs will never go over that amount. Plus Google offers some pretty extensive reports so you you'll be able to see click throughs and ad delivery. Make sure you take advantage of all reporting capabilities since it is that information that will help you decide if you need to make adjustments to your campaign. It's a great starter for a novice or a marketer that is relatively comfortable using a self driven platform in a more comprehensive campaign.

At this writing, there is a brand new option for online advertising that we're really interested in. This product is called Adneedle and it actually has the ability to trace user engagement activity beyond the stereotypical clicks. Adneedle can even track user interaction with your ad. It reports on video use, any user input at all and even mouse activity. The Adbuilder tool, which is free to use, allows you to drop and drag photos, logos, texts, incorporate a video clip or a Facebook post and you can even link up to YouTube videos. The thing we are most impressed with is how easy it is to use. You don't need any design or web coding experience to make really nice online ads. The product is just launching in a local market so check our website to find out when it will launch in your area. We think this is going to be a very popular product and we'll likely be recommending it for anyone who wants to produce their own line ads.

Okay, so that's the "boiled down" version of what web marketing is all about and how you can use it to promote your business. We're hoping you feel a little bit more confident about your understanding of how it works. However, this is a medium that is changing daily so please check our website often for updates.

Digital Media
Part B: On the Move

Next we'll examine **Mobile Marketing**. Mobile Marketing are the messages that can follow you anywhere your phone happens to be. According to a recent article from the Mobile Marketing Association, Apple has sold "only" 28 million iPhones. So basically what that means is that there are 244 million mobile phone subscribers in the US who are *not* using the iPhone. Jupiter Research, a company that helps businesses develop, extend and integrate business strategies across online and emerging channels, reports that by 2014, revenue from mobile applications will top $25 billion. Yes, you read that right. That's twenty five billion dollars! What does that mean for you? It means that there are literally millions of people who are able to receive your advertising message 24 hours a day right on their phone.

So let's start with an explanation of the simplest form of mobile message. That form would be texting. Using what is known as a **Short Message Service (SMS)**, anyone can respond to any media message at any time, regardless of their wireless carrier.

Here's how you might make that work for you. Go ahead and design a texting campaign through a digital network. Your SMS message will be assigned a six (6) digit "short code". A retail store selling blue jeans might place an SMS text **Call To Action** in their print, broadcast or online advertising. A call to action is simply asking the target audience to do something like:

> *"To get the latest sale price on CRAZYBOY Jeans,*
> *text the word 'BOY' to 654321."*

The target audience will see the ad and realize they'd be crazy not to want to receive the information. They will text to the number provided and will receive a message that says something like,

"Thanks for inquiring about CRAZYBOY Jeans. You are now one of our biggest fans."

This message lets the prospective buyer know that their information has been received and they are now in the database. All they have to do now is opt-in for offer alerts. Then they can sit back and relax as they wait for the next big sale. The next message they may see from Crazy Boy Jeans might be something like,

"For our fans only, today's sale price is $19.99. Click here to purchase or find a store nearest you."

The point of all of this is that your target audience is being directly engaged when they want to be engaged. It's a great tool for building brand loyalty.

Sounds good, right? So how do you go about placing an SMS message? Like everything else, it's really not that difficult. There are many companies out there that can assist you in your first experience into this type of messaging. One such company we're recommending right now is admob.com. There is more information about how all of this works and further recommendations on our site website. We are happy to connect you with more information and folks that can answer your questions.

The next level of mobile marketing that is available to you is the **Wireless Web** otherwise known as .mobi sites. Dot mobi sites (.mobi) are a simple way to attract the estimated 54.5 million mobile internet users to your site. You can work with your web professional to optimize your current website to be viewed in a mobile format or you might want to have a separate .mobi site that offers special incentives for users who purchase through the .mobi site.

And we're not done yet. There's more! If you are truly interested in making mobile marketing part of your media plan, you might also consider using **Mobile Banner Advertising**. It is much the same as the online digital placement we just talked about except it is delivered to mobile phones in the form of clickable ads and rich media. Beyond that, mobile banner advertising is getting more and more targeted as companies determine the best way to deliver banner ads to your cell phone. As an example let's say you're a fitness geek that likes to drink protein shakes while working out. An advertiser can deliver a message with content that will target your specific need. You could even say something like,

"Click here for a free sample today and get 20% off your next purchase."

As you're reading this you're probably asking yourself, "How many people actually bother clicking through on their phones?" Well, here's a really startling fact for you. Verizon found its mobile banner click through rate to be 2% as compared to an online click through rate of only .3%. That's right…it says "point 3".

As you consider mobile marketing, keep in mind that as is the same for other media, it is not a one trick pony. In other words, you will need a series of carefully crafted messages that together could lead to some amazing results. The key to mobile marketing is the same as all of the other planning recommendations we've shared so far. Be sure to plan, budget and benchmark your expectations.

Wow, that is quite a bit of information we've shared with you. And to make it even more interesting, it continues to change every day. So you'll need to remember several key items as you consider making digital media part of your media buying plan.

- What we have shared here is a broad approach. It would make sense to check out our site on a regular basis for specific market details. We're happy to assist you in

making decisions for your campaign.
- Everything is open for negotiation. Ask for a bargain.
- Mobile is a unique and changing technology. It makes sense to educate yourself as much as possible to stay current. A great place to get updated information besides our website is the Mobile Marketing Association website at http://mmaglobal.com/main.
- Get as local as possible. One of the great abilities of mobile marketing is geo-targeting which is reaching consumers using **Location Based Service (LBS)**. You can reach exactly the people who may be driving by your store or need your service right in your area.

So now you're a believer in web or mobile marketing or at least you feel more educated and you're wondering how you can make mobile marketing happen for your company. There are many, many companies that will be happy to assist you in getting your message onto the screens of mobile users all over the world. Check out our site at www.YourAdHereTheBook.com for an updated list of our recommendations.

CHAPTER TWELVE

Word of Mouth Marketing

These days budgets are tight and although you've set aside an advertising budget, the numbers aren't huge and you're wondering what else you can do. Fortunately, at this point in history there is so much more you can do to bring attention to your business and what you have to offer.

Social Networking, or Social Media as it is also known, is a new form of "word of mouth" advertising that allows businesses to establish relationships, and communicate in a more engaging social environment. It is free to use, however there is an established etiquette that must be followed to allow for credibility and trust.

One of the first things you're going to want to do is to join LinkedIn, which is like Facebook for businesses. It's kind of like one of those after work networking parties where you get to ask questions and collect business cards but you don't have to leave your office. It's very easy to get started. What you'll want to do is go to LinkedIn.com and set up a profile with your picture, work and employment history, and any special awards and achievements you've received. Be honest and open in your profile. LinkedIn works best if you set yourself up as a resource. Go out and answer the questions that people post. Make suggestions. Get yourself heard. Position yourself as an expert in your field by joining groups that are of interest to you and dialog with other group members. You will become a resource that people trust. Additionally, find associates, former co-workers and business contacts on the site. The majority of business owners and colleagues are already there. Ask them to write you a letter of recommendation and be sure to reciprocate by writing one for them. This process will help you build credibility in your field and that kind of credibility can really help your business grow.

Another thing you can do is have a Facebook account. Again, offer information. Are you a florist who deals in exotic flowers? Why not post information about the flowers you carry without doing a sales pitch. Maybe you're someone who collects gems and turns them into jewelry. Be creative. Think about how you can offer information. The plan is when people need the information; they will think of you and find their way to your business. This is an approach that really works.

Furthermore you can post articles and information on docstoc.com and scribed.com. This is a great way to get your information out for people to read and find you. Set up your wikipedia and post information about your business and your area of expertise. We understand how much work this is because we're doing it. But every time you post information with your name attached to it, it's one more thing that will show up about you in an internet search. Again, you're setting yourself up as an expert in your field. And yes, it is a lot of work. But it *works* and you can't beat the price.

At this writing, Twitter is becoming more and more popular. Tweeting is simply microblogging which is writing a 140 character update about what you're doing. We really need to emphasize that you be professional in your updates. You can certainly be personal and show who you are but you want your professional demeanor to come through. Here are some examples for you. Let's say you are the exotic florist that we talked about earlier. An example of a tweet you might send is,

"The new bulbs are in from Holland!"

"The optimal temperature for planting is 60 degrees Fahrenheit."

"These bulbs need a special fertilizer mix for optimum growth."

Be sure it doesn't sound like you're trying to sell something. Make it about the bulbs, not about the sale. The sales will come. Trust us when we say we see it working every single day. The objective with Tweeting is that you want people to start following your posts. All you're doing is demonstrating your passion, your excitement and your knowledge.

There are a few essentials to keep in mind. With all of the social media sites, post a current picture that you are comfortable with everyone seeing. People do business with and follow people, not icons or logos.

Update your status on a regular basis. Let people see you are actively engaged in the site.

This is social media so be social. Be careful not to just push out comments and messages. Comment and respond either publicly or with a direct message.

Don't ever spam. It's a great way to have users ignore you.

One final word of advice: *participate*. Build your profile, keep it updated and engage with the site users. It's social networking so socialize!

For more information on social media and word of mouth marketing, please check our website at <u>www.YourAdHereThe Book.com</u>. This is a rapidly changing and evolving animal and it's our passion to keep you informed.

CHAPTER THIRTEEN

Radio

Radio. It's come a long way since the early part of the 20th century when families sat in the living room to listen to President Roosevelt's fireside chats or to enjoy the latest adventures of Amos and Andy. Radio was king until the 1950's when a little invention called television came on the scene changing the world forever.

Fast-forward 50 years and radio is struggling to maintain some relevance in today's media mix. According to a radioworld.com post from March 2008, there are 13,977 licensed commercial radio stations surveyed by Arbitron, the research company that analyzes all radio stations in the United States and currently lists three hundred radio markets. Add to that the 8,321,785 subscribers and 151 stations on Sirius satellite radio and the exponential use of iPhones and other devices, we're sure you can see it is becoming exceedingly difficult for radio to rise above the clutter.

That being said, one of the greatest strengths of radio is its ability to target locally. Wherever you live, radio is a part of your community. Beyond that, because local radio does not have a long lead-time from production of your ad to the airing, it's quite easy to get your message out there quickly. Most stations also have very talented sales and promotions groups that work diligently to help you develop an event around your sale or promotion that fits with their station's target audience.

One piece of advice that we give over and over is, before you make a decision on which radio station or stations to buy, you must first consider your target audience. Although it's tempting, it's not necessarily a good idea to buy the radio station that you like to listen to. It may not be your audience. The following example should explain this clearly.

Let's say that you're a big fan of new country. You listen 24/7, you watch the Country Music Channel and you plan your schedule around watching the Country Music Awards. But you're selling high-end snowboards, mountain bikes and hiking equipment. Your inventory is completely overstocked and you want to have a big blow out sale. Right about then enters an attractive account executive from the local country station making a sales call at your business. The first thing you should do is grab this book so we can show you why it isn't a good idea to place ads on his or her station.   Be assured that he or she will have a compelling argument. But we're going to show you how to make the right choice without being influenced by station research and a cute account executive.

The first order of business when you're considering adding spot radio to your media plan is to ask yourself what is the purpose of placing the ad. Is there going to be a one-day sale? A giveaway? A chance to promote weekly specials? Always keep in mind that radio is a **Frequency Medium**; you'll need to hit listeners with your message at least 7 times before it starts to register with them. Another term you'll probably hear is **Format**. That's simply the genre or style of music the station plays.

For example, there's Country, Album Oriented Rock, Latin, Jazz, Sports/Talk, and News. Each one is a specific format. These days, most stations will have multiple formats because they belong to a *cluster* or *group* (Entercom, Clear Channel, Citadel and Infinity are some of the larger station groups).

Now let's get into some of the media measurement tools you should have at your disposal in order to negotiate with the station. The first and most basic is the coverage map that will show you the station's city of license, their wattage and signal coverage. Each piece of information is important to you as you'll want to make sure that the station message reaches your target audience. There are a number of radio station locators available for your use. We've provided a few links to maps on our website.

Before we get into the detailed measurements, we should let you know that like all other media, radio stations are analyzed on a regular basis by Arbitron. Where does the information come from that Arbitron is collecting? Well, select listeners receive what are called diaries where they will record all of their radio listening activity for the week. Those diaries are then collected and tabulated for each of the 300 radio markets and published in a research document that is made available to advertising agencies and stations four times a year. In that document is everything you always wanted to know about radio listening.

So, now you're probably wondering exactly how radio is sold. Well, just like television and cable, radio is sold based on dayparts. Those dayparts are:

- AM Drive (6A-10A),
- Mid Day (10A-3P),
- PM Drive (3P-7P),
- Evenings (7P-12A)
- Overnights (12A-6A).

These are standard dayparts but you can do a little mix and match to make your own.   Your account executive will be happy to help you figure out what will work best for you to effectively target your audience.   You can accomplish this by sending an avail request to the station you are interested in. At this time you can specify your daypart selections as well.

Next is a measure that most stations will pitch until the "cows come home". That measurement is called **Cume**. Cume is the total number of people listening in any given week. It can be thought of in a few ways but the following is an example that should make it easy to understand.

Let's say your business is located on a busy street with at least 20,000 cars passing by your storefront every week. Each one of these 20,000 cars could be a potential customer but you don't know anything about them. And this is *exactly* what the problem is when working with cume. Each and every one of those cars would be added into the number with no knowledge of who they are. Are they your target audience? Do they have any need or desire to know anything about your business? In the advertising world, this is aptly called "casting a wide net". There's quite a bit of volume provided but what is the percentage of interest?

The next measurement you'll want to understand is the **Average Quarter Hour (AQH)**. This number quantifies the number of people listening for at least five minutes in any given 15 minute period during any given daypart.

Another measurement is **Time Spent Listening (TSL)** which is important because it will tell you the length of time the audience is spending really listening. This information is useful because it will be helpful to know if listeners are tuning in for fifteen minutes or the entire day. It might make a difference in your decision to buy.

Audience Duplication is yet another measurement that you'll want to be sure to consider. Audience duplication is the measurement of the crossover or shared audience between any given station and another during a given time period. Duplication reports will help you analyze where the target audience is and will help you avoid paying a premium for something you can get at a much better rate. What we mean by this is that you might be able to get a better rate on what might be considered a station which fell lower in the Arbitron ratings. Even though it may have been rated lower, it could very well be sharing a large part of the same audience of the higher rated station. It only makes sense that you'd be paying a premium for the higher rated station and less for a lower rated station. An audience duplication report will give you some insight into who is listening whether you may be reaching your audience on the lower rated station which would in turn save you some money. It's not magic. It's just the way radio works.

Okay, so now you're armed with some details about radio and it's time to start putting your radio schedule together. The first thing to keep in mind is that *this is a negotiation.* Remember that account executive from the country station we left standing in your office door? Be sure to have him or her leave their information and tell them you're going to get back to them with a detailed request. "Leave the door open" until you're really ready to negotiate.

So let's say you are selling high-end snowboards, hiking equipment, and mountain bikes with a substantial price point. Your target audience will likely have significant disposal income and tend to be a bit younger in age.

As we mentioned earlier, you'll need to have a goal in mind for the campaign. Let's say for the sake of an example that you want to have an end of summer sale on bikes in order to make room for the incoming snowboards. You've decided that you'd like your radio ad to run for about three weeks. If the plan is to add radio to the media mix, our experience shows that you might want to consider an alternative rock station and a top 40 station. Why? Well, in general, alternative rock stations have a high time spent listening and a dedicated young male fan base that fits this product. The top 40 station balances it out for the same reasons but usually with more of a young female audience composition. However, these are broad based format generalizations and you'll need to contact the stations you're considering for your mix to request more information. If you're a little reluctant about how to find information about your market, feel free to go to our website at anytime and send us a request for your market. We'll be happy to provide you with details to help you with your radio schedule.

Your request for information should be done with an avail request form. This is explained in the availability request chapter. You can download a avail request from our website. On the form you will be providing the following information:

- **Target Demographic:** This will tell the station the age of your target group. Most target groups are broken up into 18-34, 25-54, 18-49 and 25-49.

- **Flight Dates:** These are the dates your campaign will start and stop.

- **Format:** A format is the length of time of your radio spot. Most run as 30 second spot, 15 second spot or a 60 second spot.

- **Dayparts:** As explained earlier, the daypart is the time periods during the day you would like your ad to run.

- **Average Quarter Hour (AQH) rating:** As explained, the AQH is the number of people listening for at least five minutes in any fifteen minute block of time.

- **Rate:** Rate is the cost of each spot so you'll want to be absolutely sure you get the agreed upon rate.

- **Time Spent Listening (TSL):** As explained above, TSL is the time spent with a station in a given day part noted in hours and minutes.

- **Duplication Report**: Remember the duplication report shows the audience shared between stations. You'll want to note the time period and which stations are duplicated.

- **Playlist:** A playlist is the programming that the station airs. It's completely up to you if you feel this information is important to your buy.

- **Deadline**

- **Where to send the information**

Once you send out the avail request, you will likely be inundated with phone calls and emails requesting more details. Feel free to provide as much information as you feel comfortable sharing but we urge you to use caution when it comes to sharing your budget. You'll want to maintain control. An acceptable response may be something like,

> *"We have between $5,000 and $6,000 to spend in the market."*

This will give the account executives a frame of reference for pricing.

So you've answered the questions and received the information. You're looking at what you've been provided and you decide that you're going to set your spending for this radio campaign at $2,000. Remember what we stated earlier: radio is a frequency medium and you'll need to hit listeners numerous times so that the information sinks in. We recommend a minimum of 12-15 commercial units per week. With $2,000 to spend, you'll need to focus your cost-per-spot in the $45-55 range for a 3-week period. This will keep you within your budget.

To help you to begin building your media plan, we have supplied an Excel media planning worksheet on our website. You can download the file for your use. It has been set up so that all of the dayparts and formulas are built in for you. You'll add stations to the sheet along with the AQH and rates.

As you build your plan, very possibly you'll be over the budget you set for the campaign. That's okay; it's time to start negotiating. Don't be intimidated. Be informed and have fun with it. The two areas to focus on are rate and daypart. If you want a fixed daypart, AM drive (6A-10A) for example, give that a shot first and don't be afraid to ask for a lower rate. If you're not able to make any headway there, let the account executive know that you are flexible on the daypart. He or she may be able to open up the daypart a bit. An example of opening up a daypart is widening the time period from let's say 6A-5A and from 10A-1P. You're in the driver's seat so make your expectations known and work with your account executive until you're satisfied.

If you need more help with negotiating tactics, we've provided you some tried and true tactics on our website as well as some innovative ways to get what you need. Always keep in mind that the negotiation has to be mutually beneficial. Both you and the account executive need to meet your goals or it's not going to work. So be flexible, be courteous and be ready to uncover some value added opportunities. There are many of them. You might get a show sponsorship, a weather sponsorship, web links, social networking integration and audio streams. Your account executive will be happy to talk with you about what the station has to offer.

All your hard work has paid off. You've negotiated the buy that makes the most sense for your purpose so now it's time to send an insertion order to the station specifically laying out your buy. There is a blank insertion order for your use as a download at our website. The station will sign the order and return it back to you. At this point they will let you know where to send your radio spot or in the case of the station producing your spot, they'll want your **Copy**. Copy is the message portion of your advertisement. Be involved in the production process and be sure you approve any and all copy prior to airing. Experience has taught us that by being involved, you will save all kinds of frustration and disappointment. For more information see the chapter on media production or go to our website where we discuss the steps in developing radio, TV, outdoor, print and digital creative.

So you've done it. The buy has been negotiated, the spot has been produced, the paperwork has been signed and all approvals have been made. You're finished, right? Not yet! There are some very important post buy issues that will need your attention. Be sure to:

- Request a daily spot log to see when the spots are going to run so that you can listen to them. The stations will usually have a 15 minute window for running your spot. By 15 minutes we mean it may run as early as 15 minutes or as late as 15 minutes. So tune in early and don't be upset if you don't hear the ad at exactly the time you were told. Keep listening!

- Get an **Affidavit** for any promo spots, streaming or give-aways. An Affidavit is a statement, usually notarized, that accompanies station invoices confirming that the commercial ran at the time stated on the invoice.

- Generally invoices are usually generated as soon as the last spot airs. In order to reconcile, match that affidavit to your insertion order. Any discrepancies should be adjusted immediately.

Now back to that cute account executive from the country station you've decided not to use. In this particular business scenario you'll want to say something like,

> *'Thanks so much for your information but for this campaign we decided to use WXYY FM and we would like to see how this works for us.'*

At this point, he or she will probably continue to try and make the sale. Restate your position. "Leave the door open", be respectful but firm. Radio can work if the right message is in front of the right people at the right time. Think objectively and rationally.

So there you have it…radio buying in a nutshell. If you have any questions or you're confused about any information we've provided, please feel free to contact us at www.YourAdHereTheBook.com for clarification. We are here to help and we love this stuff!

CHAPTER FOURTEEN

Print

Of all of the media opportunities we are sharing with you, print is one of the easiest to plan and buy. For the purposes of this book and to keep things a bit simpler, we'll classify daily and weekly newspapers and magazines under print publications.

As you're considering print as a possible option for your media plan, the first thing you're going to want to get your hands on is a current standard **Rate Card**. A rate card is simply a listing of current pricing. Every publication out there will have a standard rate card. You can get a copy of it either from your account executive or many will make it available right on the publication website. Go directly to the section that says "Retail Rates". It is there you will find the net rate per column inch for a display ad. Most papers will provide what is known as an **Open Rate** which simply means that it is a non-contract rate. A non-contract rate is just that; you are not asked to sign a contract and anyone using the open rate gets the same price. Another pricing concept is known as **Bulk Contract** inches. Bulk contract is an easy concept; it simply means that the more space you commit to buy, the cheaper it becomes. Additionally, there will usually be a **Combination Discount** or **Pick-Up Discount.** We don't want to confuse you with the industry definition so here's an example of what would generate a combination or pick-up discount. Let's say you want to place your ad on Tuesday and then again on Saturday. Because you'll be using the exact same ad on both days, you might be offered a 20% discount. Of course the specifics of the discount would depend on the paper you're buying but the idea is the same. And be sure to ask if there is any discount offered whenever you're placing an ad.

So far print has been very black and white (no pun intended) but now, we're going into territory where print starts to get into a little gray area. And that is…*No two papers will ever have the same dimensions for their ads.* We honestly don't know why this is, it just is. However, if you check out your favorite paper, you'll most likely see one of two formats: **Tabloid** or **Broadsheet.**

The following is an example of the way a tabloid is formatted:

- One eighth page (1/8) is approximately 7.5 column inches. You could also think of this as two columns x 3.5 inches.
- One fourth page (1/4) is approximately 15 column inches or three columns x five inches.
- One half page (1/2) is approximately 30 column inches or five columns x six inches.
- One full page is approximately 60 column inches or five columns x twelve inches.

A broadsheet format would usually be twice the size of the tabloid format; thus the name broadsheet.

Once again we want to stress that every paper is different. It would be difficult to find any two that are alike. These particular guidelines are from an area paper here in New York State and are just for example purposes. Please be sure to check with your local paper and work within their guidelines when designing your ad.

And that thought brings us to dimensions for designing your ad. So the next thing you'll want to look for on the rate card is the ad dimension mechanicals and deadlines. Unless you are a graphic designer or have knowledge of column widths, it has been our experience that it makes sense to contact the publication to ask for help prior to submitting your ad. Your question should probably be worded something like this,

> *"I'm sending you an insertion order for a 25 column inch ad. Please inform me of the exact height and width measurements so that we can send you the artwork within your specifications to avoid any problems."*

And speaking of artwork, all publications will only accept the ad via digital format either through email or an upload to a **File Transfer Protocol (FTP)** site. For those of you who don't know what an FTP site is, it is a server on the internet that maintains files for downloading. The print medium will give you the location so you can easily upload your files. Once you send the artwork and you've checked that it was received, make sure the publication sends you a proof of the finished ad for your approval before it is printed. You'll want to catch any errors before the ad runs.

The ads in your local paper are generally black and white. Be advised that there is always an extra charge for color. The price for color differential will be noted on the rate card.

Print is particularly deadline focused. You'll need to give yourself enough time to create, edit and deliver the ad. Most daily papers have a two to three day lead time while weeklies have a full week lead time. However, you'll have to check with the publication you're intending to use to get the correct deadlines for that publication.

Okay, so you've met the deadlines, your ad was proofed and ran on the schedule you requested. Remember to be sure to request what is known as a **Tear Sheet** with your invoice. A tear sheet is just that; it's a copy of your ad that has been torn out of the publication as evidence of how it ran. The tear sheet will show you exactly what the ad looked like and where it was placed in the paper. You will want to be sure to match with your order.

The final piece of information you will want from the rate card or from your account executive is the daily/weekly circulation. Publications are audited by the Audit Bureau of Circulation (ABC) and the information is provided to the papers on a regular basis. This number will tell you how many subscribers will receive the paper. Another term you will hear is readership. Simply put, readership is the circulation number multiplied by the number of average users the publication acknowledges as readers in addition to the subscriber. (Generally that number is 2.1) In other words, if a paper has a circulation of 100,000, the readership would be published as 210,000. Be cautioned that the readership number is most probably inflated. *The number you want to be concerned with is circulation.*

Depending upon your budget, you may want to consider magazines as part of your media plan. It actually is possible to have your message in well known publications like Esquire, Sports Illustrated, Newsweek, People, Forbes and Money.

Magazines will usually only accept full color, full page ads so it can be a bit on the expensive side for a local retailer. However, it's worth taking a look at because a full page, full color ad in a widely circulated magazine can build credibility and it's a great way to showcase your product or service. Here's an example of how many readers you could reach (source: MNI 2009):

- Louisville Market-Newsweek/Sports Illustrated/The Week/Time/US News & World Report
- Cost for full color/full page : $13,855
- Market circulation: 44,500 subscribers
- Impressions made: 262,860
- Cost per thousand: $311.34

(Magazines rarely talk in CPM (cost per thousand) but this is a good point for comparison.)

Deadlines for magazines range from four weeks out for weekly magazines to up to eight weeks for monthly magazines. It is important to keep in mind that *deadlines are before mail date not for cover date*. What does this mean? It simply means that a magazine like Food and Wine that has a May cover date would be delivered to your home in early April.

Like newspapers, artwork delivery will most likely be via email or FTP site and most will accept PDF formats. Be sure you check this to be sure.

As with any advertising piece, you'll want to make your message stand out. Magazines are a great way to make a rich presentation. You will get noticed. And you should consider other peripheral magazine products as well such as post it notes on an ad, barcode scans embedded on a page, gatefold format (the ads that open out of the page) and bounce back reply cards (the cards that you can tear out and send back). Each one of these options is a great way to increase your exposure.

These days newspapers are also using unique promotional tools to increase your reach. You might want to consider front page stickers, bag wraps, sampling opportunities, special events and other partnerships.

The bottom line is to know your audience and plan accordingly. Print works great to promote a special sale, event, or product launch. Let's say you've been running a spa in Birmingham and your target audience is affluent women. You could consider a full color/full page ad in the luxury categories of Cooking Light, Food & Wine, Real Simple Travel and Leisure, Town and Country.

- Ad Cost: $11,405
- Circulation: 42,460
- Impressions made: 242,500
- Cost per thousand: $268.31

In addition, you might consider adding a reply card to the ad placement to build brand loyalty by sending the reader marketing materials, directing them to a website or inviting them to a VIP event. Next, consider richly designed print ads in the City Section of the Alabama News to compliment the magazine placements.

When you come right down to it, it's all about being creative and thinking strategically when it comes to print media. If you are fresh out of ideas or want our input, go to our website at <u>www.YourAdHereTheBook.com</u> and contact us. We have a great creative team that is happy to work with you on developing with a concept that is effective.

CHAPTER FIFTEEN

Value Added

So you've got the media schedules where you want them and you've reached all of your budget and spot goals. If this is your first time around and in many cases even if it's you're 40th time around, you probably think you're done, right? Not yet! Now we're getting to the good stuff. You're going to layer your message even more with media value added sponsorships and other opportunities. We'll explain what this is and even more importantly, how you get them because you DO have to ask for them. These opportunities are a great way to get more bang for your buck.

There are a number of options that are standard for most electronic media outlets (radio, cable and television).
First of all there are open and close billboards. We don't mean to confuse you but this has nothing to do with outdoor advertising. **Open Billboards** and **Close Billboards** are the announce-

ments (audio and/or visual tags) that air just before or just after a program airs. For instance, let's go back to The Today Show. An open/close billboard is the tag before or after an ad starts that says, "Today's program is brought to you by Crazy Boy Jeans." Most media outlets will be willing to negotiate these billboards. Don't be afraid to shoot high when negotiating value added options. For instance, ask for ten (10) billboards per week. If you start out by asking for less, you'll only get less. If you start high, you'll have a better opportunity for negotiating the most exposure possible.

Once you've negotiated your value-added, all you'll need to do is provide a logo in whatever format the media needs as well as 10-15 seconds worth of text. That's it. But there is one more thing and that is to be sure you see/hear the tag for approval before it goes public. You'll want to be sure you're happy with the way it looks/sounds.

Another interesting option is a **Sponsorship**. Sponsorships are mostly reserved for radio and cable. In the area of the globe where we reside, one of the big sponsorship opportunities is for the weather. It's a popular item here because the weather changes rapidly so folks are always tuning in to determine whether they need to bring a bathing suit or a parka to the beach! The weather is a great place to be seen or heard.

A popular place in the southern US may be on a NASCAR channel, either cable or radio. Or you might want to consider specialty show sponsorships for radio. Some examples of this might be a local music show, a midday coffee break show or even a talk show about a specialty item such as pets, gardening, bicycling, etc. At this writing one of the new and interesting sponsorships comes in live streaming radio. Your ad can be heard as an audio or audio/video delivery when the station is opened. Be sure to pick wisely with your target audience in mind. These kinds of opportunities are a fantastic way to add one more layer to your ad campaign.

Another interesting sponsorship is available on cable. A tag-gable promotional mention is another great way to get noticed. We're sure you've seen them but this might be the first time you'll be able to put a name to the advertising. They are the ads you see during one show for something that will be happening later in the evening or possibly on a different day and maybe even a different channel. For example, let's say you're watching something on FX and the show goes to commercial break. There is usually a spot aired during that break urging you to tune. Those spots can be "tagged". They might say something like, "Tune into the Real World on MTV tomorrow at 8:00P. Sponsored by Crazy Boy Jeans, creating a world where there is the perfect jean for every body."

The best approach to placing taggable sponsorships is to look to your account executive for some recommendations based on your target audience. They can assist you in picking out the right taggable and crafting the appropriate message. One thing to keep in mind about this,

> *and please make a note of it so you won't be disap-*
> *pointed later on,*

you cannot dictate when these spots will run. The cable system will run them in a broad rotation through the entire intercon-nect. You can (and should) get a report of the number of promo spots that ran, where they ran and when.

Out of home advertising is a bit more fixed. Now remember that "out of home" includes billboards and any type of adver-tising that is outside. Generally the best they can offer are bonus boards. When that offer comes up, TAKE IT.

The web and mobile media have opened up a whole new arena of opportunity where you may even have the chance to design a customized sponsorship. You may get a banner delivered only to a certain geographic target, a text ad delivered to a mobile device, a 10 second forced ad that airs before an online video, a

Facebook link and live reads. It is here that your relationship with your account executive becomes vitally important. The more you share and work together, the more offers for value added options you will get. There we go with that win-win again!

Keep in mind that these are some general value added options. Check out our value added and best practices link at www.YourAdHereTheBook.com. We'll be sharing new information and opportunities on a regular basis.

CHAPTER SIXTEEN

Yellow Pages

We can't really talk about advertising without addressing the one place that almost every business has placed their very first ad. That one place is the Yellow Pages, which, of course, started with the advent of the telephone. For many people, it is an important tool in their everyday lives.

While we feel it is important to have your business name exposed to as many potential customers as possible, it may not make sense to have any paid ads in the phone book with all the other options available today. Some questions to ask before you commit your dollars are:

- Is this a service business that consumers might try to find such as a plumber, electrician, roofing contractor, a bank?
- Is this a professional medical practice, law firm or accountant?
- Are you a sports or event facility?

The question you'll need to answer is, are you viewing the yellow pages as purely a directory or are you thinking it's a good way to advertise your business? In our humble opinion, you really need to think of it as a directory only since that's how it's used by the majority of consumers. It's not a great way to build any type of awareness about your business.

For more information about advertising in the yellow pages, please check out our site at www.YourAdHereTheBook.com. We'd love to talk to you and help you make the best decision for your business regarding this type of advertising.

CHAPTER SEVENTEEN

Media Production

You sit in front of your television laughing at a message you're seeing and think to yourself, "I want to do something like that. I want an ad that makes people remember my product." Your very next thought might be, "But how the heck would I make that happen?" It's a common question; one we hear all the time. Since we're talking about electronic media (television and radio), let's start there.

In radio and television there are several standard ad size formats that you should be aware of:

- Broadcast TV and Cable: 30 seconds and 15 seconds
- Radio: 30 seconds, 60 seconds, 15 seconds and 10 seconds.

Now you need to ask yourself some standard questions. Keep in mind that these are the same questions that every marketer asks themselves before producing an ad of any type.

- Who am I trying to speak to?
- What makes my product different from others of a similar type? What is unique about this product?
- What is the message? Is this about branding myself or am I selling my product?
- How much will I need to allocate for production?
- Will I be able to re-use the creative or will it be dated?

As you might guess, television production is a bit more complicated. You'll want to consider a few options for yourself when deciding how you'd like to produce your ad.

- Do I want to use **Stock Footage?**
- Will I be shooting and/or editing with a crew?
- Will I have my cable or television station produce an ad for me?
- Will I have a pre-produced spot available into which I can insert text and **Music Beds?**

Of course bigger organizations will have a bigger budget for this type of production. But don't worry if you are a smaller business person. There are some alternatives that will get you what you need for substantially less out of pocket expense. One alternative is to have the TV or radio station produce the spot or spots for your campaign. Most will offer you a production discount or special to entice you to use their services. If you decide to take this route, there are several things you need to keep in mind.

- Most stations and cable system production companies have high quality equipment. The down side is that they are programmed to get the jobs completed quickly. They have a formula and in many cases, your ad could end up looking very much like the ad of your competitor or having the same feel of other commercials currently on the air. You won't have as much input into the creative as you might like. So before you commit to television or cable production, be sure to meet with both the account executive and the producer assigned to your account and view the reel of past ads created by that producer or check out past scripts. Try to get to know the director, producer and editor assigned to the project.

- Be clear about what you will provide and what they will provide. Are you planning to write the draft of the script and they will be finalizing it? Who will provide the music and graphics needed? Make sure you see and approve the copy of the script BEFORE production starts.

- Be certain everyone is aware of the budget. You're going to want an itemized quote from the station. Get signatures from everyone involved have before production starts.

- Be clear about whether the spot will be shot in the television studio or if you're going to want a location shoot.

- One very important item that you'll want to be sure to check is this: After the spot has been produced, can it be used on another station or will you be limited to an ad run only on the station that has produced the spot? You'd hate to put all the time and energy into producing your "new baby" and find out after the fact that you can't use it anywhere else. Generally speaking, if a TV, cable or radio outlet wrote the script and used station voice talent, you will not be able to air the spot anywhere else in the market.

- You'll want a time line. When can you expect delivery of the spot? Will it take two days, two weeks, two months? Be clear and know what you're paying for.

Another choice for producing your television spot is to use a pre-produced spot. If you decide to use this method, be absolutely sure the spot you chose is one you can easily drop in a voice over or music bed. Many will also allow you to use the text and graphics of your company to make the ad your own. There are several sites available that do a good job of pre-producing television spots. Two that we might recommend are:

- Spotrunner.com
- Adedge.com.

The process of production for a pre-produced ad is pretty much the same for each one of the above noted production companies.

- You'll complete an application or licensing agreement.
- You'll receive the ad for editing or you can request the company do the editing. Editing will include adding the voice over, texts, graphics and music bed.
- The completed ad will be shipped to the television or cable stations you have purchased.

As you browse through these sites and find you have access to all the materials you'll need to upload, you may decide that this is the best way for you to go. Most of these services are self-service and you won't have to wait long for the production to be completed which can be a bonus.

For more of these types of sites or for further questions or assistance, please check our website. We're happy to make recommendations for you.

Now of course, if you are a big company and have a large budget, you'll probably prefer to do the production work yourself. Or maybe it would make more sense for you to hire a production agency. Top notch production is expensive but on the other hand, a top notch ad will generally catch more attention than a locally produced cable spot. (Sorry cable stations!) If you're thinking you'd like to do a top notch production job yourself, we've included a Production Checklist on our website at www.YourAdHereTheBook.com.

To this point, we have covered electronic (television and radio) production. but what if your media plan also includes some web ads? The following are a few options you might want to consider.

- Adneedle.com is a digital media marketplace that will supply you the tools to create your own ads using the templates provided as well as your own graphics, texts, videos and music beds. The service is free and it's a simple drag, click and submit format. Trust us when we tell you that you do not need to have designer skills or programming ability to use this option. We mentioned earlier in the book that Adneedle is currently a local option but be sure to check in because they're expanding into other markets rapidly.

- Have the web property design your ad. If you give them the basics which include logo, color palette, video and other graphics, they should have no trouble creating a world class web ad.

- Hire a designer that is familiar with creating for the web. You'll want to be sure they know how to use the most current design software programs and that they can create based on the specifications you provide.

Feel free to contact us if you have any further questions or need help finding designers or production companies. We have many resources we are happy to share.

Glossary of Terms

Advertising Impressions: Audience delivery of media vehicles, programs or schedules. Usually expressed as thousands (000).

Affidavit: A statement, usually notarized, accompanying station invoices which confirms that the commercial actually ran at the time stated on the invoice.

Affiliate: A station associated with a network by contract to broadcast the network's programs.

Audience Duplication: Audience shared between stations.

Audit Bureau of Circulation (ABC): A non-profit circulation/auditing organization. It is one of several organizations, operating in different parts of the world, which audits circulation, readership, and audience information for the magazines, newspapers, and other publications produced by their members.

Availability Request (Avail Request) or Request for Information: Unsold units of time available for broadcasters to sell to advertisers. Also refers to a station's submission of programs and rating estimates for advertising planning and buying.

Average Quarter-Hour (AQH): The audience estimate reported by Nielsen and Arbitron for television and radio. It provides the average number of persons or households who watch/listened for at least 5 minutes of the 15 minute segment being reported.

Billboard: An outdoor advertising display. In broadcast can also be a short 5 or 10 second announcement indicating advertiser sponsorship of a program.

Bounce Back Reply Cards: A direct mail piece inserted in a magazine or other print publication.

Broadcast Calendar: An industry-accepted calendar used mainly for accounting and billing purposes. Weeks run Monday through Sunday. Each month is four or five weeks long.

Broadsheet: A newspaper in which the longer side is folded and generally is about twice the length of the longer side of a tabloid.

Bulk Contract: A discounted rate for buying print advertising in volume.

Bulletin: A larger format outdoor posting typically shown on expressways.

Cable TV: TV programming that is delivered by coaxial cable rather than over the air for the purposes of improved reception and delivery of additional program choices beyond the local stations.

Circulation: The total number of distributed copies of a publication at a specified time.

Closed Billboard: An advertising announcement after a show concludes.

Column Inch: A unit of newspaper space one column wide and one inch deep.

Combination Discount or Pick Up Discount: A print buying discount when the same ad creative is run more than one time per week.

Copy: Text or message portion of an advertisement.

Cost Per Rating Point (Cost Per Point, CPP, Cost per GRP): The cost to reach one percent of households or individuals in a given market or geographic area.

Cost Per Thousand (CPM): The cost to reach 1,000 units of audience, households or individuals for advertising. Used as a measure of efficiency among media and media schedules.

Cumulative Audience (Cume): This is another way of expressing reach. The total number of different people or households exposed to advertising at least once during the media schedule.

Daily Effective Circulation (DEC): Daily traffic count.

Daypart: The time segments into which the day is divided by broadcast media properties, determined by type or programming and who provides it (network or local).

Digital Media: A broad term used to describe new electronic media.

Drop Down Ad: An ad that when scrolled over by a mouse drops down.

Duplication: The number or percent of the target audience in one media vehicle also exposed to another vehicle.

File Transfer Protocol (FTP): A site used to exchange and manipulate files over the internet.

Flight Date: The dates an advertising campaign will start and stop.

Flighting: A technique for extending advertising dollars using periods of media activity interspersed with periods of inactivity.

Format: a) The type of music or programming genre for a radio station, b) The length of a commercial in radio or television.

Frequency Medium: Radio is often referred to as a frequency medium as it is utilized so that the audience is exposed to a message a pre-determined amount of time.

Frequency Networks: Niche cable networks that provide increased exposure.

Gatefold Format: A magazine or newspaper format that opens up to double the page size.

Gross Impressions: The combined audiences of several media vehicles or several announcements within a vehicle, leaving in the duplication among the audiences.

Gross Rating Point (GRP): The sum of individual ratings in a media plan.

Insertion Order: Written instructions from the advertiser or agency authorizing a publication to run a specific advertisement in a specific issue. Also specifies cost per ad and size of ad (in print) as well as any request for special position in a publication.

Inventory Availability: Equals the amount of spots available to purchase at a specified price in a specified time period.

Leaderboard Ad: An IAB standard format web ad. Usually stated in 160x600, 120x600 or 300x600 (pixels).

Location Based Service: Reaching consumers exactly where they are.

Makegood: Comparable unit of advertising offered at no charge when the original spot or ad did not run or ran incorrectly.

Mobile Banner Advertising: Mobile advertising targeted at mobile phones.

Mobile Marketing: Marketing on or with a mobile device such as a mobile phone. The more traditional definition is meant to describe marketing in a moving fashion such as technology road shows or moving billboards.

Music Bed: Sound or music file used to enhance a radio or TV commercial.

Net Cost: Advertising rates which do not include advertising agency commission and/or include discounts.

Open Billboard: Announcements before a program begins usually five to ten seconds in length.

Open Rate: A non-contract rate.

Outdoor or Out of Home: Advertising on billboards or signboards generally outside of a building.

Pay Per Click: A cost model implemented by search engines or other websites to charge advertisers for each time a user clicks on a specific link.

Portable Document Format (PDF): A file format created by Adobe, typically used for saving documents that are comprised of more than a simple text element.

Peel Back Ad: A rich media format that expands or contracts when clicked or moused over. Typically 100 x 30 pixels.

Per Column Inch: Print pricing term for cost of space.

Poster: The standard outdoor advertising display unit, usually 25 feet by 12 feet.

Pre-Emption: The substitution of one advertiser's local TV commercial by another advertiser paying a higher price for the spot, or by a different program of interest.

Prime Time: The part of the daily broadcast time during which the number of listeners or viewers is the highest.

Rate: Amount charged or paid.

Rate Card: A statement by a medium showing advertising costs, issue dates, program names, closing dates, requirements, cancellation dates, etc.

Rating: An estimate of the size of an audience expressed as one percent of the total population.

Reach: The unduplicated percent of a potential audience exposed to advertising one or more times during a given period.

Reach Networks: Cable networks that gather the most exposure in all targets.

Reader per Copy: Average number of readers for one copy of a newspaper or magazine.

Readership: The circulation number multiplied by the average number of users the publication acknowledges as readers.

Request for Information: Refer to Availability Request.

Rich Media: Paid web placement that my include video, music, games or other animated content.

Run of Schedule or Run of Station(ROS): A broadcast schedule where specific programs and air times have not been requested by the advertiser.

Schedule: The schedules are a plan that identifies the medial channels used in advertising campaigns. The schedules specify insertion or broadcast dates, positions and duration of the messages.

Short Message Service (SMS): A feature that allows cell phones to send and receive 160 bytes (about 160 characters) long alphanumeric messages.

Showing: A group of outdoor boards which provide a certain percent coverage of a market, usually purchased in increments of 25.

Skyscraper Ad: An IAB standard format web ad. Usually 728 x 90 pixels.

Stock Footage: Rights managed or royalty free film typically in a short format of one to five minutes.

Sweeps: The four week periods when all TV markets are measured by Nielsen and Aribitron for station viewing and demographic information. Sweep months are February, May, July and November.

SWOT Analysis: An analysis in which Strengths, Weaknesses, Opportunities and Threats of the organization are identified.

Tabloid: A newspaper that is about half the regular size.

Target Demographic: Age of a target group generally broken up into 18-34, 25-54, 18-49, 25-49

Target Profile: A statement of who make up a target audience that is consisting of age demographic, male, female or both, how target audience communicates and geographic boundary.

Tearsheet: A copy of a print ad placement used to confirm run.

Time Period: A period of time in a programming day.

Time Spent Listening (TSL): The number of minutes spent actually listening.

Traffic: A standard term that tells media outlets what copy or ad to run.

Trending: A measurement showing whether a program is losing or gaining audience.

Value-Added: Addition value at no additional cost.

Web Placement: Any paid advertising on a website.

Wireless Web: Web browser based access to the world wide web using a mobile device connected to a wireless network.

Breinigsville, PA USA
16 May 2010
238079BV00005B/7/P